Getting To Know Your Budgie

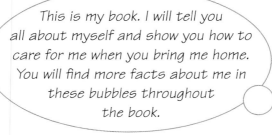

Getting To Know Your Budgie

Gill Page

INTERPET PUBLISHING

The Author

Gill Page has been involved with a wide variety of animals for many years. She has run a successful pet centre and for some time helped in rescuing and re-homing unwanted animals. She has cared for many animals of her own and is keen to pass on her experience so that children may learn how to look after their pets lovingly and responsibly.

Published by Interpet Publishing,
Vincent Lane,
Dorking,
Surrey RH4 3YX,
England

© 2001 Interpet Publishing Ltd.
All rights reserved

ISBN 1-84286-111-5

The recommendations in this book are given without any guarantees on the part of the author and publisher. If in doubt, seek the advice of a vet or pet-care specialist.

Credits

Editor: Philip de Ste. Croix
Designer: Phil Clucas MSIAD
Studio photography: Neil Sutherland
Colour artwork: Rod Ferring
Production management: Consortium, Poslingford, Suffolk
Print production: SNP Leefung, China
Printed and bound in the Far East

Contents

Making Friends	6
Getting To Know Me	8
Choosing Me	10
My Own House	12
Furnishing My Home	14
My First Day At Home	16
My Favourite Foods	18
Nice and Fresh	20
Treats and Titbits	22
Toys and Playthings	24
Taming Me	26
Time For Play	28
Safety In The Home	30
Doing The Housework	32
Keeping Fit and Well	34
Visits To My Doctor	36
Holiday Care	38
Boy or Girl?	40
My Special Page	42
Budgie Check List	43
Different Colours	44
A Note To Parents	46
Acknowledgements	48

Making Friends

Hello. I am your new friend. What is your name ? I will need a name too. I soon learn the sound of my new name. I love playing with toys. When I am sure you are a safe friend to play with, I will come out of my cage to be with you. I want you to talk to me. I may even learn to talk to you. I will need fresh food and water every day.

If you train me, I will learn to eat from your hand.

I will be very young when I first come to live with you, so I will need lots of time to rest. I sleep at night, but I don't have a bed as you do. I sit on my perch, tuck my head under my wing, and go to sleep. I keep my feathers looking smart. I don't have to be brushed, but you can help by giving me a shower using a plant sprayer filled with cold water. I have wings and so I need to fly to keep fit. If I am living in the house, you must train me and then I can fly around in your room. I have a strong beak to help me eat. I can also use it to bite if you scare me, so please be kind.

We will soon become good friends.

Getting To Know Me

I am a budgerigar, but budgie is much easier to say. I have green feathers, but there are lots of other colours from which you can choose. Many budgies are blue – some have white feathers on their faces and others have yellow. A lot of my friends have grey feathers. Budgies that only have white feathers are called "albino". They have red eyes and pink feet too. The "lutino" has all yellow feathers, except for its tail, wing tips and patches on its face – these are white. Others are a mix of colours.

We are great friends and chatter to each other all day. If you want me to learn to talk, I must live in a cage on my own.

Only pick me up when you really have to. I do not like being held as it makes me nervous, and I might get frightened and accidently peck you.

I eat seeds and some plants. I can be a bit noisy at times, but so can you! I will be very lonely if I have to stay on my own for a long time. Be sure to talk to me before you go to school and we can chat again when you come home. Leave a radio on; I can listen to it while you are out of the house. If you need to hold me, you must be very careful not to hurt me. Put one hand over my back, with my head between your first and second finger. Gently cup your other hand around the front of my body so that I am held securely.

Choosing Me

You can buy me from a pet shop or from someone who breeds budgies at their home. I must be about six weeks old. It is much easier to train me when I am young. If I am an older budgie, I may never learn to sit tamely on your finger. When you come to choose me, you should look at me carefully. You will be able to tell if I am young. At six weeks old I will have all my grown-up feathers. I will have thin black stripes across the top of my head, down to the top of my beak. My eyes will be bright and shiny and my feathers will be clean, especially round my bottom – it's a bit rude but I won't mind if you peek quickly. If my cage, and the food and water pots, are clean, I should be healthy.

Ask the owner to catch me. Feel my chest – it should be plump. If you can feel a bone sticking out, I am too thin. This can mean that I am ill or that I have not learned to eat my seed. Choose a fatter friend. I must travel home in my very own carry box.

Take me home with you in a special cardboard box or carry case. Because I need fresh air, they will have ventilation holes in them.

My Own House

I would like my home to be ready for me to move into straight away. I like a *big* cage. A long one is best, not a tall skinny one. I fly forwards, not up and down like a helicopter. I like climbing, so please make sure that some of the bars stretch from side to side of the cage. The bars must not be more than 10mm (0.4in) apart. I am sure to get my head stuck if they are.

My new house will probably have ready-made perches in it, but I like it if you also cut some branches from a fruit tree for me. I can chew these as well as sit on them. I like my cage to be set quite high off the ground – I feel safe there. I don't like to be near the window in summertime. Phew! much too hot. I hate draughts too. It easier to tame me in a cage this size, because I can't fly too far away. When I am really happy with you, I could have a really big cage. This is called an aviary. It is made of wood and wire. It is so big that you can stand in it too. Buy one from a pet shop or ask a grown-up to build one for you.

I like wooden perches best, not plastic ones. You can make extra perches for me from willow, hazel or apple twigs.

Furnishing My Home

In my home I will need a food bowl and something to hold my water. A water fountain is best – this is a long tube that holds water. I can drink from the small dish at the bottom. I cannot make the water dirty when I use a drinker like this. Be sure to change the water often – I don't like the taste of stale water. Use one of these tubes for my seed as well. I prefer a dish that has a perch on it as this makes it easier for me to eat. It is the same when you sit at the table to eat your meals.

To keep the bottom of the cage clean you can use sand sheets, loose sand or lining paper and wood shavings. (Only use shavings that are sold specially for me and other pets.) I also need a pot for my grit. I must have grit to eat. I do not have any teeth and the grit grinds up the seed in my tummy.

I would like a clip to secure my fresh food and my cuttlefish to the bars of the cage. I also need a bird bath. Washing keeps my feathers in good shape. Choose one that hangs in the doorway of my house so I will not make a mess of the cage floor when I am splashing about in it.

Bird sand

Sand sheet

Shavings

My First Day At Home

I will be very scared when I first come to live with you. When we arrive, just pop my little carry box into my new house and open one end of it. When I am safely sitting on the perch, you can take my box away. Cover half the cage with a towel so that I will have somewhere to hide. Make sure that I can reach my food and water easily. Put the bowls near the perch, not directly under it or I will make a mess in the food. Check that I am eating normally. If, on the first day, I don't seem to be eating out of my dish, hang a spray of millet near to me. That's a real treat.

I will grow to be about 18cm (7in) long, and can live for 10 years or more.

For the first few days try not to stare at me. It worries me. Quietly check my food bowl every day and talk to me while you are doing it. I can hear very well, so keep talking. You can't see my ears – they are hidden under my feathers. You can put your hand flat against the cage. I will become used to seeing you there. Always look away from me as you do this. After two weeks I should be used to you. Now you can begin training me. I'll tell you about that on page 26.

Look away from the cage while you to get to know me, so that I don't get frightened.

My Favourite Foods

I am a seed eater. You can buy food that is made just for me. It is a mixture of different seeds. I crack open the seeds with my beak, spit out the outer shell (called the husk) and eat the inside. Every day you must take away all those empty husks. If you are feeding me from a pot, just puff onto the top of the bowl and this will blow all the husks away. If you are using a food hopper, put your finger over the hole, take the top off and tip out the little dish. Then put it all back together. When the bowls are nearly empty, tip the last few seeds out and put fresh seed in.

I will need the seed, grit, iodine block and cuttlefish in my cage to keep me healthy. The water fountain helps to keep my drinking water clean.

Grit

Cuttlefi

Seed

Water fountain

Iodi bloc

I love gnawing away at hard things like this cuttlefish or my iodine block. It helps to keep my beak in good shape.

I have already told you about my grit bowl, but sometimes you can put some extra grit into my seed bowl. Then you will be sure that I am eating the grit that I must have. There are two other things that I need to stay healthy. One is cuttlefish. It keeps my beak short and is good for my bones. Another is a mineral, or iodine, block. This also helps to keep my beak in trim and gives me the extra vitamins I need.

Nice and Fresh

There are other things I should eat to keep me feeling good. Like you, I must eat my greens and fruit. Before you give me anything to chew, check that it is fresh and clean. You don't like eating anything that is smelly and slimy, do you? Vegetables that I can eat are carrots, watercress, celery, spinach and even corn-on-the-cob. Apples, pears and grapes are good. Blackberries are yummy, but wash them well before you give them to me. I cannot eat a whole apple or pear – just a slice will do. Throw away any bits that I don't eat in one day.

I love to eat millet – it's my favourite – but only give me one millet spray a week.

Spinach leaves

Carrot

Grapes

Pear   *Apple*

  You can even pick weeds from the garden for me. I just love nibbling groundsel, chickweed and dandelion leaves. Don't forget to wash anything that you pick, will you ? Ask a grown-up to check that you have picked the right plant and not one that might harm me. Another food that I just adore is a millet spray. It is such a treat that I may only want to eat the millet, and nothing else. One millet spray a week is enough. Only give me a teeny weeny piece of vegetable, fruit or greens at first. I can eat more as I grow bigger.

Treats and Titbits

Do you like sweet treats? So do I. But too many are bad for us. I must only have one sweet treat a week. You can buy my treats from pet centres. Some look like a bumpy stick. Hang it in my cage. The one I like best is honey and egg flavour. Some are shaped to look like a bell. I keep thinking it is going to ring as I eat it! If you watch when I am eating, you will soon see which treats I like best. Like you, there are some I love and some I don't like at all.

Sometimes the treats are good for my health. Add a drop or two of cod liver oil to my seed. There are other drops that have lots of different vitamins in them. Always read the label on the bottle before you put anything into my food. Ask a grown-up for help if you need to.

Apple-flavoured beak block

Kiwi fruit seed stick

Bell-shaped honey and seed treat

Feeding Timetable

Breakfast
Blow the husks off the surface of the seed. Is there enough for me to eat during the day? Pop in my piece of vegetable, fruit or greens.

Supper
Check my seed again. See that my water is clean. Take out any fresh food that may be left over.

Toys and Playthings

I am really quite clever you know, and I get very bored if I am left on my own with nothing to do. Lots of toys keep me happy. I like room to fly in my cage, so don't put too many toys in at one time. It is much more fun if you change my toys around every week or so. I do like a mirror in my house all the time. When I look into it I think it is another budgie friend. I will talk to the mirror for hours.

I love to climb my ladder. Sometimes it has a bend in the middle with a toy put there, and I enjoy turning it round with my beak. Some toys fix onto the perch. I bash these with my beak and make a lot of noise. Some toys can go on the floor of my cage. These will need washing every day. A bell is good fun, but I may be too noisy – then you will have to take it out of the cage. You don't have to buy all my toys; you could make some yourself.

Empty cotton reels tied together with strong string make a cool toy. A fir cone is great too. I can really tear that to bits!

I love climbing. I will use my beak as well as my toes to help me climb my ladder. My toes are very strong, I can even hang upside down from my perch. Don't you think I am clever?

Taming Me

Taming me will take time and lots of kindness. You must be very quiet. You look so big to me that I'll be quite frightened to begin with. Start by placing the flat of your hand against the cage. Put some of my favourite food into my bowl. When I am nibbling it, slowly put your hand into the cage and stroke my feathers with one finger. When I am used to that, you can go on to the next stage. Stroke the front of my chest with your first finger. Put your finger at the bottom of my chest, in front of my legs. Gently push against my legs and I should put one, or both, of my feet onto your finger. Let me step off again whenever I want.

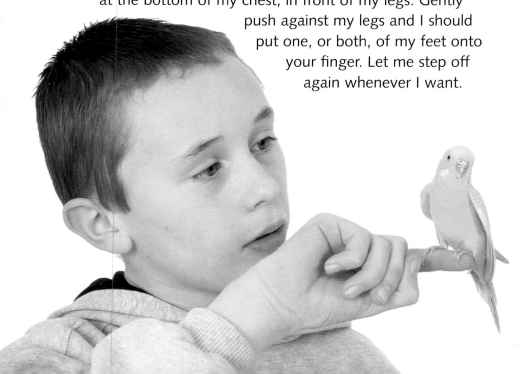

My long tail helps me to balance when I perch and steers me when I am flying.

Keep doing this every day until I am quite happy sitting there. Then you can lift me out of the cage on your finger. You can let me fly around the room for some exercise. Remember to shut all the windows and doors. Close the curtains and cover mirrors so that I won't bump into them. Block any fireplaces. Whee! I'm off. When you want to put me back into my house, just let me hop onto your finger and pop me inside.

Time for Play

Now that I am finger-tame, there are lots of things we can do together. From your finger you can pop me onto your shoulder. I will enjoy sitting on your head. I can preen your hair in the same way as I do my feathers. I am very nosy. Make sure there is nothing in the room to harm me.

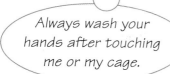

Always wash your hands after touching me or my cage.

Do not have any hot drinks in the room. I could burn my toes if I try to sit on the edge of the cup or mug. Roll a wooden or plastic ball along the floor. We could play our own sort of football game. When I am out of my cage, keep saying my name. If I fly to you, give me a treat as a reward. I will enjoy this and I will soon learn to come when you call. I may also learn to say my own name. Do you want me to speak other words? Just keep saying one word over and over again to me. When I have learned that word you can try another one. Do not be upset if I do not learn to speak. Some us never learn how to do it.

Safety In The Home

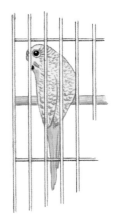

Please make your home safe for me to play in. Never let me out of my cage until you have checked that all the doors and windows are closed. If I escape out of the house, you will never find me again. I will not be able to find any food and the weather outside will probably be too cold or too hot. Other birds will gang up on me and hurt me. Other pets and wild animals can kill me. Do not have any of your other pet friends in the same room as me when I am flying around.

We will stay safely in here, while you clean out our cage.

Make sure the windows are shut before letting me out of my cage.

Never leave me alone in the same room as your cat and dog friends, even if I am in my cage. They could try to attack me and knock the cage over.

I like to be in a smoke-free zone. Aerosol sprays make me very ill if used near me. Some houseplants are poisonous, so take them away before letting me wander outside my cage. Even if the plants are harmless, I will chew them, so it is best to take all plants away.

Sometimes I may be naughty and will refuse to go back into my cage. Turn any lights off, throw a duster or tea towel over me and pick me up gently in it.

Doing The Housework

I know I make an awful mess in my house, but I do like you to keep it clean and tidy. Every day you must clean out the bottom of my cage. If I have a sand sheet, just throw the old one away and put a new one in. If I have sand or shavings, scoop out the dirty bits.

Take out my food and water when spraying the cage with disinfectant.

Every week the cage will need a good scrub. First put me into my special carry box. This keeps me safe while you are cleaning my house. Throw away the sand sheet, sand or shavings. Put on some rubber gloves and wash the tray with warm, soapy water. Rinse and dry it with a paper towel. Spray it with my pet disinfectant. Leave it to dry. Take everything out of the cage. Wash the bars with a wet cloth and spray them with a little bit of the disinfectant. While the cage is drying, wash out my food dishes and water fountain. You will have to use a bottle brush to clean inside the water bottle. Wash all the perches and all my toys. When everything is dry, put it all back together. Refill my seed and water pots. Then you can put me back. Oh yes, that looks nice!

Keeping Fit and Well

I cannot tell you if I am not feeling very well. You will need to check me to see that I am fit and healthy. Look at my feet. My nails can grow too long. If they are curling right under my toes, the vet will have to clip them for me. The vet will also trim my beak if it is overgrown. I don't like having it done, but it doesn't hurt. Give me lots of things to chew and my beak should stay the right length. Those are easy things to check.

I don't really like having my claws cut, but the vet is always kind, and never hurts me.

Ask a grown-up to help you check for other things that are harder to spot. I may catch something called "scaly face". I can get it on my legs as well. If the skin on my legs or around my beak looks crusty and flaky, you must buy something to treat it. The vet or pet shop will help you. My cage must not sit in a draught because, like you, I can catch a cold. You will see me wheezing, with a runny nose and eyes. This is bad news. Take me to the vet at once. If I am not feeling very well, I will sit on my perch with my feathers all fluffed up. The vet will tell you what is wrong with me.

If I need to take medicine you can put a few drops into my food.

Visits To My Doctor

My doctor is called a veterinary surgeon. Vet for short. I am not very keen on my visits to the vet centre, but the vet is always very kind and gentle with me. Take me in my special carry case. Take my cage too. The vet can see where I live at home. By looking at the cages, vets can spot signs that help them cure our illnesses. The vet will give you medicine for me if I need it. I must visit my vet once a year for a health check. I will be looked at from top to toe. My wings and feathers will be checked for damage and the presence of mites. These are horrid insects that bite me and spoil my lovely feathers. The vet will give you medicine to kill them. Just talking about them makes me feel itchy.

Health Check List

1 Look at my eyes – are they bright and shiny?
2 Check my beak and nostrils – are they clean and smooth?
3 Do my claws need cutting?
4 Look at my tail feathers – are they clean?
5 When I am really tame, you can weigh me. Just line the scales with kitchen towel and sit me on them. Write down my weight each week. You soon see if I am getting too fat.

A vet will look at my wings to make sure I do not have mites.

Holiday Care

I need somebody to take care of me every day. If you are going on holiday, you must find a friend you can trust to look after me. Before you pack your suitcase, you must get mine ready. I will need enough food to last the time you are away. I always prefer eating the same sort of seed mixture. Don't forget my grit. You must also pack my sand sheets or shavings. You could even pop in some twigs for extra perches. How about some new toys? They will give me something to play with while you are away.

Help your friends by making a list of what I do and don't like.

Make a list of all the things that must be done for me every day. If your friends haven't looked after pets like me before, show them how I like things done. I think it would be safer for me to stay in my cage all the time you are away. I can have extra long flying time when you are home again. Take me to your friends the day before you go away. This will give them a chance to telephone you if they have any questions about looking after me. Leave them my vet's name and telephone number too.

I hope she remembers to pack our treats and all our favourite toys. Do you think she will send us a postcard?

Boy or Girl?

It is much more fun for me if I have a friend to keep me company. With two budgies to look after, it is even more important that you tame us. We will need to stretch our wings regularly. It is unkind to keep us cooped up in a cage all the time. It's best to have two girls or two boys living together, but it does not matter too much if you have a girl and a boy. We almost never have babies unless you put up a nest box specially.

Can you see the bump at the top of my beak? This is called the cere. My cere is brown and that tells you that I am a girl.

Our ceres are blue. Now that we are grown up, you can tell that we are both boys.

How can you tell if I am a girl or a boy? All budgies have what is called a "cere". It is a sort of hard, waxy swelling at the top of my beak. When I am a baby, it is hard to tell what I will be. As I grow older, my cere changes colour. If I am a boy, my cere will become bright blue. If I am a girl, it will turn dark brown. It is harder to tell if I am an albino or a lutino (an all-yellow budgie). Their ceres do not turn bright blue. In that case, ask an expert to tell you whether I am a girl or a boy.

My Special Page

My name is ~~SNOWY~~ - OSCAR

My birthday is 6 weeks
1-3-2008

Am I a boy or girl?

Boy ?

My colour is

White with small amout of Blue.

Died 23/7/2013
3.30pm

My favourite fruit is CARROT

My favourite toy is MIRROR

My favourite treat is ? millett - Spinach.

How long is my tail?   2 ins   2"   3/4" ?
                       6/3/08   17/4   8/1/2012

My vet's telephone number is 02392 668 916

HARBOUR VETERINARY HOSPITAL
251 · London Rd. Northend PO2 9LA
VETS NOW are open 24 hours a DAY 365 DAYS A year

Health check done 12/3/08   spoke JANEY 2015   0845 223 2610 Emergency NO.